Enslow Publishing

INVESTIGATE!

WHO'S THE GREATEST? Sports Stars

SHOHEI OHTANI VS. BABE RUTH

KATHLEEN CONNORS

BASEBALL'S GREATEST

Please visit our website, www.enslow.com. For a free color catalog of all our high-quality books, call toll free 1-800-398-2504 or fax 1-877-980-4454.

Library of Congress Cataloging-in-Publication Data

Names: Connors, Kathleen author
Title: Shohei Ohtani vs. Babe Ruth : baseball's greatest / Kathleen Connors.
Other titles: Shohei Ohtani versus Babe Ruth
Description: Buffalo, New York : Enslow Publishing, [2026] | Series: Who's the greatest? Sports stars | Includes index.
Identifiers: LCCN 2025036085 (print) | LCCN 2025036086 (ebook) | ISBN 9781978547025 library binding | ISBN 9781978547018 paperback | ISBN 9781978547032 ebook
Subjects: LCSH: Ohtani, Shohei, 1994—Juvenile literature | Ruth, Babe, 1895-1948–Juvenile literature | Baseball players–United States–Statistics–Juvenile literature | Baseball players–United States–Biography–Juvenile literature | Baseball players–Japan–Biography–Juvenile literature | LCGFT: Biographies
Classification: LCC GV865.O42 C66 2026 (print) | LCC GV865.O42 (ebook) | DDC 796.357092–dc23/eng/20250815
LC record available at https://lccn.loc.gov/2025036085
LC ebook record available at https://lccn.loc.gov/2025036086

Published in 2026 by
Enslow Publishing
2544 Clinton Street
Buffalo, NY 14224

Designer: Tanya Dellaccio Keeney
Editor: Kristen Rajzak Nelson and Therese Shea

Photo credits: Cover (Ohtani) Cal Sport Media/Alamy Images; cover (Ruth) M Bill Waterson/Alamy Images; p. 5 (Ruth) https://upload.wikimedia.org/wikipedia/commons/1/13/Babe_Ruth2.jpg; p. 5 (Ohtani) https://upload.wikimedia.org/wikipedia/commons/e/e6/Dodgers_at_Nationals_%2853677192000%29_%28cropped%29.jpg; p. 7 https://upload.wikimedia.org/wikipedia/commons/6/6d/Babe_Ruth_-_St._Mary%27s_Industrial_School.JPG; p. 9 https://upload.wikimedia.org/wikipedia/commons/9/9e/Babe_Ruth_Red_Sox_1918.jpg; p. 11 https://upload.wikimedia.org/wikipedia/commons/a/af/Ohtani_batting_2019.08.04%283%29.jpg; pp. 13, 15, 19, 21, 23 Conor P. Fitzgerald/Shutterstock.com; p 14 https://upload.wikimedia.org/wikipedia/commons/5/51/Babe_Ruth_by_Bain%2C_1919.jpg; p. 17 Courtesy of the Library of Congress; p. 20 https://upload.wikimedia.org/wikipedia/commons/5/5b/Babe_Ruth_Warm_Up_Swing.png; p. 22 https://upload.wikimedia.org/wikipedia/commons/9/9f/Babe_Ruth_c1922_by_Underwood_%26_Underwood.jpg; p. 24 https://upload.wikimedia.org/wikipedia/commons/1/11/1920_Babe_Ruth.jpg; p. 25 https://upload.wikimedia.org/wikipedia/commons/a/a5/Dodgers_at_Nationals_%2853677091634%29.jpg; p. 26 https://upload.wikimedia.org/wikipedia/commons/d/db/1920_Babe_Ruth_by_Paul_Thompson.jpg; p. 27 https://upload.wikimedia.org/wikipedia/commons/8/81/Dodgers_at_Nationals_%2853676737176%29.jpg; p. 29 (Ruth) https://upload.wikimedia.org/wikipedia/commons/thumb/0/09/Babe_Ruth_Plaque_commons.jpg/500px-Babe_Ruth_Plaque_commons.jpg?20070912172449; p. 29 (Ohtani) Image of sport/Alamy Images.

Printed in the United States of America

CPSIA compliance information: Batch #CW26ENS: For further information contact Enslow Publishing, at 1-800-398-2504.

CONTENTS

Words in the glossary appear in **bold** type the first time they are used in the text.

COMPARE THE GREATS

Babe Ruth and Shohei Ohtani started playing **professional** baseball almost exactly 100 years apart. For much of Ruth's **career**, there were only 16 teams in Major League Baseball (MLB). Today, Ohtani plays in an MLB made up of 30 teams. There are many other differences between how baseball is played today and Ruth's time on the field.

Even with these differences, we can try to compare these baseball greats. Then, you'll decide: Who's the GOAT?

Did You Know?

GOAT stands for "greatest of all time."

BABE RUTH

SHOHEI OHTANI

BOTH RUTH AND OHTANI PLAYED PITCHER AT TIMES DURING THEIR CAREERS.

MAKING OF THE "BABE"

George "Babe" Herman Ruth Jr. was born in Baltimore, Maryland, on February 6, 1895. His parents, George and Kate, had eight kids. However, only Ruth and his sister Mamie lived to be adults. The family had little money.

Ruth got into a lot of trouble as a kid. He skipped school and stole things. His parents sent him to a special school known for its **discipline**. It was there that Ruth learned to play baseball.

Did You Know?

Stories about Ruth often say he was an orphan, or a child without parents. That's not true, though his mother died in 1912 when Ruth was a teenager.

RUTH HAD A HARD LIFE BEFORE HE BECAME A BASEBALL PLAYER.

Ruth got to be so good at baseball that one of his teachers brought in Jack Dunn, the owner of the Baltimore Orioles, to see him play. The Orioles were a minor league baseball team. Dunn signed Ruth after watching him play for just an hour!

Ruth played for the Orioles starting in 1914. It was here that Ruth earned his famous nickname. Ruth was called Jack Dunn's new "babe" by either his teammates or a writer—and the name stuck!

Did You Know?

Ruth was a tall man at that time. He was more than 6 feet (1.8 m) tall.

BY JULY 1914, RUTH AND TWO OTHER ORIOLES HAD BEEN SOLD TO THE RED SOX, THE MLB TEAM IN BOSTON, MASSACHUSETTS.

OHTANI'S START

Shohei Ohtani was born on July 5, 1994, in Oshu, Japan. Both he and his brother started playing baseball when they were kids.

By high school, Ohtani was playing pitcher. He became known for being able to throw fast and hard. When he was just 17, he could throw a ball 99 miles (159 km) per hour! This and his height—6 feet 5 inches (1.96 m)—got Ohtani noticed by baseball scouts worldwide.

Did You Know?

In sports, a scout is someone who goes looking for new, exciting players.

OHTANI'S FATHER PLAYED BASEBALL AT A HIGH LEVEL TOO. HE PASSED ON HIS LOVE FOR THE SPORT TO HIS SONS.

After high school, Ohtani wanted to head right into playing professionally for an MLB team in the United States. However, he was chosen first in the 2012 Nippon Professional Baseball (NPB) **draft** by the Hokkaido Nippon-Ham Fighters, a professional Japanese team. The team told Ohtani that playing for them would help prepare him for playing on an MLB team. So, he signed with them.

Ohtani got even better as he played for Nippon-Ham. He gained muscle and started hitting incredible home runs. In 2016, Ohtani led his team to the championship!

Did You Know?

MVP stands for "most valuable player."

1.86 ERA (BEST IN NPB IN 2016)

PACIFIC LEAGUE AND JAPAN SERIES CHAMPION (2016)

PACIFIC LEAGUE MVP (2016)

OHTANI PITCHED AS WELL AS HIT AS THE DESIGNATED HITTER (DH) FOR NIPPON-HAM.

FIRST MLB SEASONS

Ruth made his MLB debut on July 11, 1914. However, after five games, he was sent to a minor league team—which he led to the International League pennant! Ruth was back with the Red Sox in 1915, succeeding with an 18-8 record. By 1916, he had the best ERA in the league.

RUTH PITCHED FOR THE RED SOX AS WELL AS PLAYED FIRST BASE AND OUTFIELD.

1.75 ERA (1916)

SET THE SINGLE SEASON RECORD FOR HOME RUNS (29 IN 1919)

Did You Know?

In 1916, Ruth set the record for most shutouts thrown by a left-handed pitcher with nine. The record still stands, though it was tied by Ron Guidry in 1978.

All 30 MLB teams wanted to sign Ohtani when he was ready to do so in 2017. He went to play for the Los Angeles Angels. His play delivered! He hit 22 home runs and started 10 games on the mound.

OHTANI CHOSE TO PLAY FOR THE ANGELS PARTLY BECAUSE IN THE AMERICAN LEAGUE, HE COULD PITCH AND HIT AS A DESIGNATED HITTER. THE MLB IS MADE UP OF THE AMERICAN LEAGUE AND NATIONAL LEAGUE.

MLB ROOKIE OF THE YEAR (2018)

RUTH ON THE YANKEES

In December 1919, Ruth was sold to the New York Yankees for $100,000. That might not sound like a lot of money compared to what athletes make today, but it's this time of Ruth's career that most baseball fans picture when they think of the Babe!

With the Yankees, Ruth began to change the game of baseball. Instead of slowly gaining hits to move players around the bases, Ruth would hit a homer and send everyone home!

Did You Know?

Ruth played outfield with the Yankees.

YANKEES ALL-TIME HOME RUN RECORD (659)

YANKEES ALL-TIME BATTING AVERAGE (.349)

YANKEES SECOND ALL-TIME RBIS (1,971)

YANKEES THIRD ALL-TIME HITS (2,518)

RUTH PLAYED 15 SEASONS WITH THE YANKEES. WHEN HE **RETIRED** IN 1935 (AFTER A SEASON WITH THE BOSTON BRAVES), HE HELD MANY YANKEES **FRANCHISE** RECORDS.

DODGER TIME

Ohtani was a standout on the Angels. In the 2021–2022 season, he started 23 games as pitcher and had 156 strikeouts. The next season he had 219 strikeouts in 28 starts! By 2023, Ohtani had established himself as an incredible MLB hitter too.

Then, Ohtani became a free agent. He signed with the Los Angeles Dodgers in December 2023. His 10-year contract was for $700 million, the biggest amount in professional sports up until then.

Did You Know?

A free agent is an athlete who is not under contract with any team and is able to join any other team they like.

OHTANI SET FRANCHISE RECORDS FOR BOTH THE ANGELS AND THE DODGERS. AND, AS HIS CAREER IS ONGOING, HE'S LIKELY TO SET MORE!

ANGELS RECORD FOR HIGHEST WIN PERCENTAGE FOR A PITCHER (.667)

ANGELS EIGHTH ALL-TIME HOME RUN HITTER (171)

DODGERS SINGLE-SEASON HOME RUN RECORD (55 AS OF SEPTEMBER 2025)

IN THE MLB

During Ruth's career, he led the league in **slugging percentage** 13 times! He was the top in RBIs five times and home runs 12 times. It's no surprise that at the time he retired, he held 56 MLB records!

SOME OF RUTH'S RECORDS HAVE STOOD THE TEST OF TIME, SUCH AS THE MOST RUNS SCORED IN A SINGLE SEASON. OTHERS HAVE SINCE BEEN BROKEN.

MLB RECORD FOR MOST RUNS SCORED IN A SEASON (177 IN 1921)

MLB RECORD FOR TOTAL BASES IN A SEASON (457 IN 1921)

MLB ALL-TIME LEADER IN SLUGGING PERCENTAGE (.690)

Ohtani has put his name in the MLB record books as well as the two franchises he has played for. In September 2023, he became the first player to hit 50 home runs and get 50 steals in a season.

OHTANI FINISHED THE 2024 REGULAR SEASON WITH A TOTAL OF 54 HOME RUNS AND 59 STOLEN BASES.

FIRST 50-50 SEASON IN MLB HISTORY (2024)

Did You Know?

Ohtani had elbow **surgery** in September 2023. So, in his first season for the Dodgers, he didn't pitch at all.

MVPS

Ruth is known as a great player today, but his talent was recognized when he was playing too. He was very popular with fans and made the Yankees a must-see team. In 1923, a new Yankee stadium opened. People called it the "House That Ruth Built."

ONE-TIME MLB MVP (1923)

RUTH WAS ONLY NAMED MVP ONCE—BUT NOT BECAUSE HE WASN'T THE BEST IN THE LEAGUE. IT'S BECAUSE AMERICAN LEAGUE PLAYERS WERE ONLY ALLOWED TO WIN IT ONCE AT THAT TIME!

Ohtani has been recognized for his incredible play too. He has been named as an All-Star as both a pitcher and designated hitter. When he first achieved this in 2021, he was the first player in history to be named an All-Star as both a pitcher and a position player!

TWO-TIME AMERICAN LEAGUE MVP (2021, 2023)

NATIONAL LEAGUE MVP (2024)

FIVE-TIME MLB ALL-STAR (2021, 2022, 2023, 2024, 2025)

OHTANI IS ONE OF THE BEST PLAYERS ON THE MLB FIELD TODAY.

Did You Know?

The MVPs of both the American League and National League in the MLB are chosen by a vote among people in the Baseball Writers' Association of America.

THE WORLD SERIES

Ruth won multiple World Series titles with two teams. Three of his big wins were with the Red Sox. The other four he won with the Yankees. In addition, Ruth led the Yankees to win seven pennants, or American League championships.

TODAY, THE WORLD SERIES CHAMPION WINS THE BEST-OF-SEVEN GAMES. HOWEVER, AT TIMES DURING RUTH'S CAREER, THE SERIES WAS BEST-OF-NINE GAMES.

SEVEN-TIME WORLD SERIES CHAMPION (1915, 1916, 1918, 1923, 1927, 1928, 1932)

Did You Know?

The pennant winners of the National League and American League face off in the World Series.

Ohtani played well for the Angels, but the team never made it to the postseason. And in his first season with the Dodgers, the team did! In fact, Ohtani and the Dodgers made it all the way to the World Series—and won in game 5 against the Yankees!

WORLD SERIES CHAMPION (2024)

OHTANI IS ONLY THE 14TH PLAYER IN BASEBALL HISTORY TO WIN BOTH A WORLD SERIES AND A JAPAN SERIES.

HOME RUNS

Ruth was the first MLB player to hit 30 home runs in a season—and 40 and 50! After he started playing, the number of home runs hit in baseball increased over the whole league. In 1927, Ruth hit 60 home runs, a record that stood for 34 years.

714 CAREER HOME RUNS

RUTH IS THIRD ON THE LIST OF ALL-TIME MLB HOME RUN LEADERS. BARRY BONDS IS NUMBER ONE WITH 762 HOME RUNS DURING HIS CAREER.

Did You Know?

Roger Maris broke Ruth's home run record in 1961, hitting 61 homers.

Ohtani is known for hitting home runs. But he's also outstanding at just getting hits. As of September 2025, he has 1,050 career hits as well as more than 665 RBIs. What will his stats look like in a few years?

280 CAREER HOME RUNS (AS OF SEPTEMBER 2025)

WE CAN'T COMPARE OHTANI'S CAREER HOME RUNS WITH RUTH'S UNTIL HE'S DONE PLAYING BASEBALL FOR GOOD.

GREATS OF DIFFERENT ERAS

Ruth was in the first group of baseball players to be inducted, or invited, into the Baseball Hall of Fame in 1936. In 1948, his number 3 jersey was retired by the Yankees too. Not long after, Ruth died on August 16, 1948.

Ohtani's **legacy** is still being created on the field today. If he continues playing like he has, it's likely he's headed for the Baseball Hall of Fame too. Can he reach the heights of the Babe?

MORE THAN 350 PLAYERS HAVE BEEN INDUCTED INTO THE BASEBALL HALL OF FAME. OHTANI IS ON HIS WAY TO JOIN RUTH THERE!

GLOSSARY

career: The job someone chooses to do for a long time.

discipline: A kind of strict training.

draft: The process of selecting new players for a league.

ERA: Earned run average. The number of earned runs allowed by a pitcher, divided by the number of innings pitched, then multiplied by 9. The lower the number, the better.

franchise: A professional sports team that is a member of an organized league.

legacy: Something that is passed down from someone.

professional: Earning money from an activity that many people do for fun.

RBI: Runs batted in.

retire: To leave a job.

rookie: First year player.

slugging percentage: The number of bases a batter gets from his hits divided by his opportunities at bat.

surgery: A medical treatment used for injuries and illnesses that involves operations.

FOR MORE INFORMATION

BOOKS

Buckley, James. *A Kids' Guide to the National Baseball Hall of Fame: The Greatest Players from Hank Aaron to Derek Jeter to Cy Young*. New York, NY: becker&mayer! Kids, 2024.

Streeter, Anthony. *World Series All-Time Greats*. Mendota Heights, MN: Press Box Books, 2025.

WEBSITES

Babe Ruth
baberuth.com
Find out everything you want to know about baseball great Babe Ruth.

Shohei Ohtani, Stats, Age, Positions
www.mlb.com/player/shohei-ohtani-660271
Check out all of Ohtani's latest stats on the official MLB website.

INDEX